Chocolate
Australian Icons

Volume 1

Real Letters, Real Companies, Real Funny!

Neil Cameron

DEDICATION

To Mother Moi.
By far the best mum I've ever had.

Mondelez International
Consumer Advisory Service
Cadbury
PO Box 1673
Melbourne
VIC 3001

Neil Cameron
PO Box 6163
Yatala
QLD 4207

07-07-2014

Dear Cadbury

This has caused lifelong distress.

I have never eaten a Caramello Koala, nor will I. The thought of biting the head off one of Australia's most treasured animals, (chocolate or furry), just horrifies me. And! When has a Koala ever worn a t-shirt, pants and shoes?

Other countries do not have endemic animal shaped chocolates. Do you think China has chocolate Pandas? Africa has chocolate Monkeys? Iceland has chocolate Ptarmigans? Canada has chocolate Beavers? Of course not. It is just Australia. Why must you exploit them so? Please explain your philosophy on Caramello Koala and why you think it is okay to feed children chocolate Australian icons.

Thank you for your time. I look forward to hearing from you.

Yours sincerely

Neil Cameron

Mondelez Australia Pty Ltd
ABN: 78 004 551 473

Consumer Advisory Service
Level 6, South Wharf Tower
30 Convention Centre Place
SOUTH WHARF VIC 3006
Australia

GPO 1673, Melbourne VIC 3001

T: 1800 003 275
mondelezinternational.com.au

July 30, 2014

Mr Neil Cameron
PO BOX 6163
YATALA QLD 4207

Dear Mr Cameron,

Thanks for contacting us about our Cadbury Caramello Koala product.

Caramello Koala has been a much loved chocolate treat for children and adults alike for over three generations and we appreciate you taking some time out of your day to provide us with your feedback and concerns.

Your comments have been forwarded to our chocolate team for their information and if we can be of assistance in the future please do not hesitate to contact our Consumer Advisory Service on free call 1800 250 260.

Yours sincerely,
MONDELEZ INTERNATIONAL

Sarah Viliamu

Sarah Viliamu
Customer Solutions Specialist

Ref # 1038852

Consumer Advisory Service
Cadbury
PO Box 1673
Melbourne
VIC 3001

Neil Cameron
PO Box 6163
Yatala
QLD 4207

08-08-2014

Dear Ms Viliamu

It actually took me MOST of the day to write. Almost certainly because I have a weakness for using full-stops. But whatever, keep cramming them hairy iconic confectionary figures down the progenies! Aussie Aussie Aussie!

Yours sincerely

Neil Cameron

Complaints Dept
Reckitt Benckiser
Aerogard
44 Wharf Road
West Ryde
NSW 2114

Neil Cameron
PO Box 6163
Yatala
QLD 4207

07-06-2014

Dear Aerogard

I live a naturist lifestyle, (most weekends). However, because of my body-type I do not belong to any club or group, (also I am not a pervert). So I camp in the bush.

This is actually the problem — insect bites. Aerogard really burns the bejesus out of my genital area.

I am sure some time ago I read some literature that your company was to produce a product for sensitive skin. Did this ever eventuate?

Something needs to be done because at the moment I only have two choices – either a burning penis or an itching penis.

Yours sincerely

Neil Cameron

Reckitt Benckiser
HEALTH · HYGIENE · HOME

3 June 2014

Mr Neil Cameron
P.o. Box 6163
YATALA QLD 4207

Dear Mr Cameron,

Thank you for your contact regarding our Aerogard® products, and can appreciate your situation.

At this time there has been no specific product developed for use in the genitals area, and confirm that the Aerogard® products are not to be used in the genitals area.

If have any queries, please do not hesitate to call Consumer Services on Australia 1800 022 046.

Yours sincerely

Daniel

Consumer Relations
RECKITT BENCKISER Pty Ltd
Australia & New Zealand

Ref No. R056437580

Reckitt Benckiser (Australia)
Pty Limited
ABN 17 003 274 655
Trading as Reckitt Benckiser
44 Wharf Road
West Ryde NSW 2114 Australia
PO Box 138
West Ryde NSW 1685
T +61 2 9857 2000

www.rb.com

NEIL CAMERON

Aeroplane Jelly Head Office
71 Fairbank Road
Clayton
VIC 3169

Neil Cameron
PO Box 6163
Yatala
QLD 4207

10-07-2014

Dear Aeroplane Jelly

I am the newly elected President of 'The Jelly Club'. We get together bi-monthly for safe adult fun.

The 'Jelly Room' is a constant feature at all our functions, (it is always the most popular room, wink wink). We hire a portable Hot Tub and fill it with your Lime Jelly. Unfortunately our annual membership fee will now only cover the Tub hire and jelly for the first five events of the year.

Our longest serving member, who we all affectionately call Long John, (nudge nudge), suggested at the AGM we contact you. To see if you would consider sponsoring our Christmas function, (held over three days in December), i.e. some free Lime Jelly! Or could you offer us a bulk discount?

Hope you can help us out!

Yours sincerely

Neil Cameron
P.S You are more than welcome to come join us. (Bikini optional, wink wink)

Hi Neil,

RE: Donations for your Fund Raising Activities Letter.

As you can well appreciate we have many requests for donations. As such we have had to develop a policy that unfortunately must be fairly stringent in its interpretation.

Aeroplane Jelly has agreed to sponsor or donate foods to organisations, schools, etc. whose projects are involved in and around our local community. Many of our workers come from the surrounding area and it is to these causes that we contribute.

Please accept our apologies for not being able to support you with your efforts but wish you all the best in your endeavours.

Yours Sincerely

Nancy Clement

Customer Service Officer

McCormick Foods

Aeroplane Jelly Company, 63 Fairbank Road, Clayton South, Victoria 3169 Tel: 9264 0833 Fax: 0546 9198

NEIL CAMERON

Akubra Hats
PO Box 287
Kempsey
NSW 2440

Neil Cameron
PO Box 6163
Yatala
QLD 4207

20-05-2014

Dear Akubra Hats

Look we have a problem. I have just bought myself yesterday what I thought was one of your western style hats — 'The Bobby', off a Chinaman, (a black one).

My mate Dave reckons it is a fake! He reckons because the fur on it runs in a clockwise direction, (like cats etc). He reckons Akubra bunny hats run in an anti-clockwise direction.

Sounds ridiculous! I think my mate might be pulling my beak! Is he?

What do you reckon?

Yours sincerely

Neil Cameron

25th July 2014.

Mr. N. Cameron,
P.O. Box 6163,
YATALA, QLD 4207.

Dear Neil,

Thank you for your letter regarding the black Bobby hat.

Our Managing Director, Stephen Keir, has asked if at all possible could you could take photographs of both the inside and outside of the hat so he can let you know one way or the other.

If this can be done could you please email them to me at jenny@akubra.com.au

Hopefully your beak will be perfectly safe!

With kind regards,

Jenny Newham.

AKUBRA HATS PTY. LIMITED | Incorporated in NSW | ABN 62 000 175 333
South St, South Kempsey NSW 2440 Australia | PO Box 287 Kempsey NSW 2440 Australia
phone: 02 6562 6177 | fax: 02 6562 8726 | email: akubra@midcoast.com.au | web: www.akubra.com.au

Nestle Australia
Allen's Lollies
Consumer Services
GPO Box 4320
Sydney
NSW 2001

Neil Cameron
PO Box 6163
Yatala
QLD 4207

08-05-2014

Dear Allen's Lollies

My problem is the snakes. Specifically their length. They vary in length greatly. I have a rare form of O.C.D that concerns food. All food must be uniform in length. It just has to be that way. I cannot give you a reason why. Uniformity is very important to me. I would go mad if not for uniformity.

Can you programme your robots to cut the snakes exactly the same length? Boy this would help me so much!

Thanks for hearing me out. Hard to talk about. Please let me know.

Yours sincerely

Neil Cameron

Nestlé Australia Ltd.
ABN 7 000 011 316

CONSUMER SERVICES
1 HOMEBUSH BAY DRIVE, RHODES NSW 2138
POSTAL ADDRESS:
GPO BOX 4320, SYDNEY NSW 2001

TELEPHONE.   1800 025 361
E-MAIL: consumer.service@au.nestle.com
FACSIMILE: 61 2 9736 0407
OUR REF: 0018783370

27 May 2014

Mr Neil Cameron
PO BOX 6163
YATALA QLD 4207

Dear Mr Cameron

Thank you very much for your contact and comments about ALLENS Killer Pythons.

We appreciate hearing from our consumers as your reactions to our products contribute to our decision-making.

We hope you will continue to use and enjoy our products and we will keep your thoughts on file for future reference.

Yours sincerely,
NESTLÉ AUSTRALIA LTD.

Sandra McKeon
SENIOR CONSUMER SERVICES ADVISER

Privacy Note - Your personal information is held in accordance with our Privacy Policy which is available www.nestle.com.au. Nestlé has committed to not collect any data from children under the age of 15 If you are under the age of 15 please contact us on 1800 025 361

Nestle Australia
Allen's Lollies
Consumer Services
GPO Box 4320
Sydney
NSW 2001

Neil Cameron
PO Box 6163
Yatala
QLD 4207

23-07-2014

Dear Allen's Lollies

Awesome! I just heard the news on the radio. You are going to cut all the snakes the same size! Thank you for doing that especially for me. Very rare these days that the customer gets heard. Usually they just get sent a generic copy and paste style letter. That has absolutely nothing to do whatsoever with the subject at hand! Many trees give their lives and for what? Pointless ink and twaddle.

Thanks again for going the extra mile, (exactly a mile though, any further and that would have freaked me right out).

Yours sincerely

Neil Cameron

Arnotts Biscuits Ltd
Tim Tams
24 George Street
North Strathfield
NSW 2137

Neil Cameron
PO Box 6163
Yatala
QLD 4207

20-05-2014

Dear Arnotts

Everyone is born different. Some have Asthma, nut allergies, diabetes etc. Lots of people have phobias- spiders, tall buildings, rats, small spaces etc as well. We are even different colours. Myself, I do not like rectangles. We are all different. But that is why the world is like it is.

Have you ever thought of making square 'Tim Tams'? You could cut the ones in half you make now and keep the same packaging. They would be bite sized then and not terrify me.

What do you think of my idea about square 'Tim Tams'? Hope you write to me soon with the good news. Thank you Arnotts.

Yours sincerely

Neil Cameron

4 June 2014

Mr Neil Cameron
P O Box 6163
YATALA QLD 4207

Dear Mr Cameron,

Thank you for contacting us regarding our Arnott's Chocolate Tim Tam biscuits.

We work hard to make sure we meet our consumers' expectations and provide them with the quality and taste they have come to expect of our products. For example, we are continually talking to consumers to seek their feedback on our existing product range, opportunities for further improving our products and concepts for new ideas.

You may like to know we have something like our Tim Tam Chocolicius Bite Size biscuits on the market. They are available in two flavours; Tim Tam Original and Tim Tam Dark Chocolate, plus previously we also made Tim Tam minis.

Thank you again for taking the time to get in touch with us and providing your feedback.

Yours sincerely,

Dragica Nikolic
Consumer Contact Representative
Ref.   2014230510/DN

CONSUMER CONTACT CENTRE

Arnott's Biscuits Limited ACN 008 435 729
Registered Office: Level 1, Building B, 24 George Street, North Strathfield NSW 2137
Postal Address: Locked Bag 55 Silverwater, Sydney NSW 2128 Australia
Telephone: 1800 24 24 92 (Toll Free) Facsimile: 61 2 8767 7856
Visit our website at www.arnotts.com.au

Arnotts Biscuits Ltd
Tim Tams
Dragica Nikolic
24 George Street
North Strathfield
NSW 2137

Neil Cameron
PO Box 6163
Yatala
QLD 4207

12-05-2014

Dear Dragica

Tim Tam "Bites"? I went and bought some, as per your instruction. Guess what Dragica? I ended up at the Emergency Department, the Emergency Department! Rectus Angulas! Equiangular quadrilaterals! Quadrilaterals with four right angles! Rectangles Dragica, bite-sized rectangles! Cold Arnott's Consumer Contact Rep, cold!

Yours squarely

Neil Cameron

P.S I think your time would be better spent helping your husband Tomislav run Serbia rather than trying to earn a few extra Dinar's moonlighting as a sadistic "Australian" Consumer Contact Rep.

RSPCA Australia Inc
PO Box 265
Deakin West
ACT 2600

Neil Cameron
PO Box 6163
Yatala
QLD 4207

25-05-2014

Dear RSPCA

Visualise this. Lebanese neighbours on the left, Lebanese neighbours on the right.

The ones on the right are a big problem, (do not get me wrong RSPCA the left ones are also a problem, just not so much). I have been hearing a strange animal noise coming from their back shed. It started last week.

I do not know exactly what a camel sounds like so I went on 'You Tube' on my computer. That is the noise in the shed!

So yesterday I spotted one of them going into the shed, so I waited. When he slinked back out I shouted at him — *"Hey is that a camel in your shed? You cannot keep a camel in your shed over here mate!"* (I do not think so anyway?). You know what he yelled back? *"Mind your own* (swear word) *business Aussie!"* Which was pretty insulting either way I look at it.

My mate Dave says I will start a war and I am surrounded by them. So this is the reason for writing a letter first. What can we do about this camel RSPCA? Are there laws about keeping camels in your back shed?

Yours sincerely

Neil Cameron

RSPCA
for all creatures great & small

Neil Cameron
PO Box 6163
Yatala
QLD 4207

Dear Neil,

Thank you for contacting RSPCA regarding your concerns.

In Queensland, RSPCA Inspector's work within the parameters of the Animals Care and Protection Act which does not have provisions regarding noise complaints. Complaints regarding noise would be best directed to the local council as these are issues that are addressed in their local laws. Your local council will also be able to advise regulations/laws in relation to keeping a camel on a residential block.

To enable a complaint to be lodged with the RSPCA, you would need to provide your welfare concerns for the animal. If you can see that the animal is in poor condition, has an injury or has no shelter/food/water etc an RSPCA Inspector would be able to attend the address and assess the animal's welfare. To put a complaint through you need to have seen the animal and supply the current situation/concern regarding the animal and the animals address. We could also require some details from you, such as name, address and phone number.

It is RSPCA's procedure that complainants information is kept confidential, we only ask for it in order to gather further information if required and to verify the complaint. However, if you would prefer you can make an anonymous complaint, although keep in mind that we cannot stop the owner from guessing who made the complaint regardless of whether you leave your details with us or not.

If you could please forward more information to cruelty_complaints@rspcaqld.org.au, or call our call centre on: 1300 852 188.

Kind regards,

Clare Gordon
Cruelty Complaints
Administration Officer
RSPCA Queensland

The Royal Society
for the Prevention of
Cruelty to Animals
Queensland Inc.

ABN 74 851 544 037

Animal Care Campus

139 Wacol Station Road
Wacol QLD 4076

Locked Bag 3000
Sumner Park BC QLD 4074

P 07 34 26 99 99
F 07 38 48 11 78
E admin@rspcaqld.org.au
W rspcaqld.org.au

Animal Care Centres

Bundaberg
Doblo Street
West Bundaberg QLD 4670
P 07 41 55 17 49

Cairns
Arnold Street
East Stratford QLD 4870
P 07 40 55 14 87

Dakabin
Goodwin Road
Dakabin QLD 4503
P 07 38 86 03 57

Gympie
Launceston Road
Gympie QLD 4570
P 07 54 82 94 07

Kingaroy
Warren Truss Drive
Kingaroy QLD 4610
P 07 41 62 55 01

Noosa
Hilliti Road
Noosaville QLD 4666
P 07 54 49 33 71

Toowoomba
43 Vanity Street
Toowoomba QLD 4350
P 07 46 34 13 04

Townsville
69 Tompkins Road
The Bohle QLD 4818
P 07 47 74 51 30

RSPCA

HELPING ANIMALS • ENLIGHTENING PEOPLE • CHANGING LIVES

NEIL CAMERON

The Hon Tony Abbott PM
Parliament House
Canberra
ACT 2600

Neil Cameron
PO Box 6163
Yatala QLD 4207

20-05-2014 & 07-07-2014

Dear Prime Minister

I know you are a busy bloke cycling and running the country. But look I am not one to pick up pen and paper at the drop of a hat. This is pretty important Tony. So one I need you to read this and two I need you to tell me what you can do to put it right.

The National Sports Teams are attired in "Australian Gold" coloured Uniforms. Seriously Mr Prime Minister who is kidding who here? "Australian Gold!" It is yellow and it is yellow all day long. They, (the uniforms), are as yellow as Noah Crowe's nicotine stained fingers, as yellow as Greg & Trev's backs in 81, as yellow as Dixon Street, as yellow as Boony's liver, as yellow as a Vegemite label, as yellow as Coon Cheese. The Netball Diamonds look like a pack of cheap highlighters from 'Officeworks'.

What needs to happen is a standardised colour, (that is gold in colour and nothing like yellow), needs to be decided on for all of Australia's National Uniforms. You must be able to implement something with all your power? This needs to be taken very seriously. It is very important. The world is watching, (and quietly sniggering). Thank you for your time. I look forward to hearing from you Tone.

Yours sincerely

Neil Cameron

Australian Government

Department of the Prime Minister and Cabinet

ANDREW FISHER BUILDING
ONE NATIONAL CIRCUIT
BARTON

Reference Number: C14/48691

Mr Neil Cameron
PO Box 6163
YATALA QLD 4207

Dear Mr Cameron

Thank you for your correspondence dated 20 May 2014 to the Prime Minister.

The Prime Minister has asked me to thank you for your correspondence.

Your views are noted and they are important. A strong democracy and a responsive government always require constant feedback from its people about the issues that concern them.

The matters raised in your correspondence relate to the portfolio responsibilities of the Minister for Sport. As such, the Prime Minister has referred your correspondence for a response.

Further details about contacting the Minister and department can be found at www.gold.gov.au.

Thank you again for writing to the Prime Minister.

Yours sincerely

Ministerial and Parliamentary Support Branch

1 7 JUN 2014

Postal Address: PO BOX 6500, CANBERRA ACT 2600
Telephone: +61 2 6271 5111   Fax: +61 2 6271 5414   www.pmc.gov.au   ABN: 18 108 001 191

Australian Government

Australian Sports Commission

Ref No: MC14-007839

Mr Neil Cameron
PO BOX 6163
YATALA QLD 4207

Dear Mr Cameron

Thank you for your correspondence of 20 May 2014 to the Prime Minister, the Hon Tony Abbott MP regarding Australian sporting team uniforms. As the matter lies within the Minister for Sport's portfolio, your letter has been referred to me for a response.

Since the late 1800s, green and gold have been popularly accepted as the national sporting colours, both locally and around the world. In 1984, green and gold were formally recognised as Australia's national colours by the then Governor-General Sir Ninian Stephen.

While I understand your comments about Australian uniforms being more yellow than gold, it should be noted that the colour gold formally recognised by the Governor-General is Pantone 116C, which is a golden yellow as seen at http://www.pantone.com/pages/pantone/colorfinder.aspx?c_id=199.

Australian sporting teams are generally unrestricted in their use of the national colours with green and gold able to be used in any design or arrangement of colour, as long as it emphasises the green or gold.

More information on Australia's national colours is available at
http://www.itsanhonour.gov.au/publications/symbols/factsheets/national_colours.pdf.

I trust that this information is of assistance.

Yours sincerely

Steve Jones
General Manager
Corporate Operations

July 2014

T 61 2 6214 1111   Leverrier Street Bruce ACT 2617   /theais
E info@ausport.gov.au   PO Box 176 Belconnen ACT 2616   /ausport
ausport.gov.au

AIS

Australian Government

Department of the Prime Minister and Cabinet

ANDREW FISHER BUILDING
ONE NATIONAL CIRCUIT
BARTON

Reference Number: C14/63854

Mr Neil Cameron
PO Box 6163
YATALA QLD 4207

Dear Mr Cameron

Thank you for your correspondence dated 7 July 2014 to the Prime Minister.

The Prime Minister has asked me to thank you for your correspondence.

Your views are noted and they are important. A strong democracy and a responsive government always require constant feedback from its people about the issues that concern them.

The matters raised in your correspondence relate to the portfolio responsibilities of the Minister for Health. As such, the Prime Minister has referred your correspondence for a response.

Further details about contacting the Minister and department can be found at www.gold.gov.au.

Thank you again for writing to the Prime Minister.

Yours sincerely

Ministerial and Parliamentary Support Branch

18 August 2014

Postal Address: PO BOX 6500, CANBERRA ACT 2600
Telephone: +61 2 6271 5111 Fax: +61 2 6271 5414 www.pmc.gov.au ABN: 18 108 001 191

NEIL CAMERON

The Hon Tony Abbott
Prime Minister
Parliament House
Canberra
ACT 2600

Neil Cameron
PO Box 6163
Yatala
QLD 4207

27-08-2014

Dear Ministerial & Parliamentary Support Branch Person with the chicken scratch styled signature (good for you, stuff them).

Whatchoo talkin bout Willis? Obviously the colour is more puke yellow than Australian Gold, but Minister for Health? Whom I believe to be the former root vegetable Peter Dutton? I imagine he will get overly excited about the Dixon Street reference, which is exactly why he is the last person to sort out a colour problem!

I was just pulling your left tit about Boony's liver, also nobody really cares about Russel Hood and his grubby fingers.

Yours sincerely

Neil Cameron

McCain
Ring Road Wendouree
PO Box 105
Wendouree 3355

Neil Cameron
PO Box 6163
Yatala
QLD 4207

15-06-2014

Dear McCain

Sometimes I think advertising companies over-ride their clients to make them look stupid, (who knows why, probably just for fun).

Out here in the real world we are so sick of hearing that you have - *"Done it again!"* You sell frozen food stuffs. It is not really ground-breaking you know.

Maybe I am missing the point? (It happens mate). What have you *"Done again?"* Frozen more food stuffs? Why not change it? Here is one — *"We keep doing it!"*. Nowhere near as annoying or patronising, (and free).

Let me know A.S.A.P what you think of my catch phrase *"We keep doing it!"*. She is a beauty.

Yours sincerely

Neil Cameron

Australia Zoo
Croc Section
1638 Steve Irwin Way
Beerwah
Queensland 4519

Neil Cameron
PO Box 6163
Yatala
QLD 4207

02-07-2014

Dear Australia Zoo

G'day, look I have some problems and some questions for you guys.

So awhile back I was away fishing, (barra), and I found a baby croc. At first I thought it was a snake. You know why I thought it was a snake? Because it had no legs, chewed off by something. It was near enough dead. Maybe I should have left him, but I took him with me instead.

So anyway, I cleaned his wounds and looked up the computer what to feed the little guy and that is what I did. I call him Neville. Do not know why but for some reason it suits him. He can get a round, not that fast, he goes good on the grass but the kitchen floor is another story. There is a little pond out back and he can swim pretty good if I am honest.

When I walk the dog he comes with us. I pull him along on a skateboard. Most people laugh which I do not like. It is not funny that Neville has no legs.

So you can see my problem I wrote about earlier. He is going to get big. I can probably extend the pond and have an old surf board that I can put wheels on. He gets on good with the dog, (mostly). So no worries there. Should I be feeding him chickens yet? Are the frozen ones from Coles going to be okay? How often does he need a chicken? What else should I feed him? Or just stick with the frozen chickens? Any other advice? Have you come across this before?

NEIL CAMERON

You guys know crocs so hope you can help me with Nev.

Yours sincerely

Neil Cameron

Australia Zoo,
Croc Section,
1638 Steve Irwin Way,
Beerwah, Q 4519

Neil Cameron
PO Box 6163
Yatala, Q 4207

Friday 25th July 2014

Hi Neil,

Thanks for your letter. This certainly is an unusual situation but demonstrates how tough crocs can be. We have found adult crocs missing limbs in the wild on many occasions. In reality this croc should be returned to the area he came from. It sounds like you have got him over his injuries so he should be ok from that perspective if he's in an area with plenty of water.

It is not legal to keep crocs as pets in Queensland and as you say he is going to grow very large. I also don't think permission would be granted to keep him in captivity. The best place for him I would suggest is back in the wild in the area he came from.

Kind regards,

The Croc Team

Open everyday 9.00am - 5.00pm | 1638 Steve Irwin Way | Phone +61 7 5436 2000 | info@australiazoo.com.au
Closed Christmas Day, ANZAC Day open 1.30pm - 5.30pm | Beerwah Sunshine Coast Qld 4519 | Fax +61 7 5494 8604 | australiazoo.com.au

NEIL CAMERON

Australia Zoo
The Croc Team!
1638 Steve Irwin Way
Beerwah
Queensland 4519

Neil Cameron
PO Box 6163
Yatala
QLD 4207

13-08-2014

Dear The Croc Team

I think I will take my chances with Neville. Actually thinking on it further if I play my cards right, (and accidently on purpose kick out a couple of fence palings), he could potentially sort out my camel infestation problem.

Keep up your good crocodile work.

Yours sincerely

Neil Cameron

Clarks Rubber
Support office
Admin Building
254 Canterbury Road
Bayswater
VIC 3153

Neil Cameron
PO Box 6163
Yatala
QLD 4207

01-05-2014

Dear Clarks Rubber.

What rubber or maybe foam would work as a sound deadener on a shed? Is it better to stick sound deadener inside the shed you want to sound deaden or on the outside walls of the shed you want to sound deaden?

My mate Dave saw a thing on You Tube with egg cartons. They just used a glue gun. But that is a lot of eggs and it is not my shed.

What is best do you think? Hope you can help me out.

Thank you.

Yours sincerely

Neil Cameron
P.S Do you know if camels would eat foam or rubber?

Clark Rubber Franchising Pty Ltd ACN 065 708 723

Clark Rubber Franchising Pty Ltd
Administration Building, 254 Canterbury Road Bayswater Victoria 3153
Telephone: +61 3 8727 9999 Facsimile: +61 3 9729 3266
franchising@clarkrubber.com.au

www.clarkrubber.com.au

26 May 2014

Neil Cameron
P O Box 6163
Yatala Qld 4207

Dear Neil,

Thank you for your letter regarding Sound foam.

We do sell Acoustic Foam sheets that can be adhered to your walls.
I would think it would be best to place them on the inside of the shed.

If you contact Clark Rubber Southport at 07 5561 1333 or Clark Rubber Browns Plains at 07 3806
6911, they would be able to assist you in purchasing.

Sorry I am not able to assist you regarding the camels.

Regards

Steve Fatileh
Rubber Category Manager

Labor Leader
PO Box 6022
House of Representatives
Parliament House
Canberra ACT 2600

Neil Cameron
PO Box 6163
Yatala
QLD 4207

28-06-2014

Dear The Hon Bill Shorten

This will never reach your desk, I know that.

I see you got all the hair and no glasses unlike your brother Bob, but his legs are longer, way longer. So it evens out. When you become Prime Minister, you will join Frank Forde. Which will be a record either way you look at it. Good work on that front Bill.

Just some advice for you Bill. Get Chloe more involved. She is particularly photogenic and the same height. Check how Tony takes advantage of his hot daughters. His kiwi Mrs is used less often. Helen Clark is also a kiwi. You get where I am coming from on that score?

What is your stance on Immigration? Lebanese and kiwis coming over to live? Maybe your PA will slip this on to your desk. But I doubt it. I saw you pretending to shop at Big Sam's once. You should have bought some lifts?

Good luck Bill.

Yours sincerely

Neil Cameron

NEIL CAMERON

Office of the Leader of the Opposition

16 July 2014

Mr Neil Cameron
PO Box 6163
Yatala QLD 4207

Dear Mr Cameron,

Thank you for your correspondence regarding Labor's immigration policy.

The contribution that migration has made to Australia needs to be properly acknowledged. We are a nation built on migration. The fabric of Australian society is richer from the experience of migration, including the contributions of those Australians who came here as refugees or asylum seekers.

The issue of those seeking asylum in Australia is very complex. It has been estimated that there are 7 million people around the world who are seeking permanent asylum. Australia's humanitarian program provides for 13,750 places. But even if we offered 100,000 places – which no political party advocates – we would still be saying "no" to millions of worthy refugees. That is the wicked dilemma which underpins this area of policy.

Precisely because of this complex dilemma, before we discuss the precise measures Australia takes in order to reduce the sum of global misery, we need to be very clear about our values.

Values that drive modern Labor are compassion, fairness and generosity underpinned by a fundamental maxim: that as a country we should not harm people.

Compassion leads us to seek an end to the loss of life at sea. The Regional Resettlement Arrangement (RRA) that was put in place by the Labor Government last year with Papua New Guinea has played a key role in saving lives at sea and we continue to support this measure. But it does not absolve the Abbott Government from their obligations to ensure the Manus Island and Nauru detention facilities are places that are safe, humane and dignified. The key finding of the Cornall Report into the tragic incidents at the Manus Island detention facility in February made it clear that the failure to process or resettle those in the facility was the major cause of these disturbances. The fact that there was no discussion between Minister Morrison and his counterpart in PNG about resettlement demonstrates the Abbott Government dropped the ball on the RRA and the Manus Island detention facility.

If we are to bring about an end to the loss of life at sea, Australia also needs to work cooperatively with our regional neighbours to ensure we have a sustainable regional solution to the long-term irregular movement of people.

PO Box 6022 Parliament House, Canberra ACT 2600 • Tel:(02) 6277 4022 • Fax:(02) 6277 8592

Fairness leads us to empower the United Nations High Commissioner for Refugees (UNHCR) in helping us make the choice of who should qualify for our humanitarian program, rather than people smugglers.

Fairness also leads us to think about the way we treat people who are already here. We should not be treating those already in Australia in a mean spirited way by putting them on temporary protection visas (TPVs). TPVs only create an endless cycle of limbo, despair and dependence, serve no deterrent value and are costly.

Generosity leads us to increase our humanitarian intake. We are a rich country and we must be doing more as a key global player in the UNHCR framework.

Labor will continue to consult widely on this complex issue in the coming months.

Thank you for writing with your concerns.

Yours sincerely

Office of the Leader of the Opposition

NEIL CAMERON

The Hon Bill Shorten
Labor Leader
PO Box 6022
House of Representatives
Parliament House
Canberra ACT 2600

Neil Cameron
PO Box 6163
Yatala
QLD 4207

30-07-2014

Dear unknown Opposition Leaders Office letter opener/copy and paste person who also sounds like they may have over-staying neighbours

Strewth! Ease up there Sharon!

I must admit, I cannot recall seeing too many kiwi boat-people on the news paddling across the Tasman seeking Asylum. Where are you people getting your information from? Pauline Hansen?

Let me know Sharon, this is big.

Yours sincerely

Neil Cameron

Billabong
1 Billabong Place
Burleigh Heads
QLD 4220

Neil Cameron
PO Box 6163
Yatala
QLD 4207

10-06-2014

Dear Billabong

My wife bought me some of your big shorts yesterday. I am not interested in surfing or the beach as I am allergic to most sand. I have been allergic to it since I was born. That is okay though, I hate the beach. So it worked out well for me in the end.

Anyway the shorts my wife bought. I have never worn shorts like them before. My wife says it is okay to wear giant beach shorts even though I do not go or like the beach. When I put them on I feel like I am wearing a uniform. Not a nice uniform either, like The SS. I do not mean The Silver Surfer either.

Maybe if you, (Billabong staff), say it is okay to wear the big Billabong shorts and to stop feeling like it is a uniform then that may very well help me out with this problem. They were not cheap and she has gone and lost the receipt. I am not a rich man, which she knows.

Yours sincerely

Neil Cameron

GSM (Operations) Pty Ltd
ABN 67 085 950 803
Trading as Billabong Australia

1 Billabong Place
Burleigh Heads QLD 4220
Australia

PO Box 283
Burleigh Heads QLD 4220
Australia
Tel +61 7 5589 9899
Fax +61 7 5589 9800

Sydney
Retail Office
2/192 Harbord Road
Brookvale NSW 2100
Australia
Tel +61 2 9458 4900
Fax +61 2 9939 8600

Queensland
Sales Office
PO Box 283
Burleigh Heads QLD 4220
Australia
Tel +61 7 5507 9399
Fax +61 7 5507 9300

South Australia
Sales Office
5 Vincent Avenue
Somerton Park SA 5044
Australia
Tel +61 8 8294 3500
Fax +61 8 8294 3600

Victoria & Tasmania
Sales Office
PO Box 434
Torquay VIC 3228
Australia
Tel +61 3 5261 1099
Fax +61 3 5261 4719

Western Australia
Sales Office
Unit 2/29B Selby Street North
Osbourne Park WA 6017
Australia
Tel +61 8 9382 5800
Fax +61 8 9382 3788

www.billabong.com.au

Hi Neil,

Thank you for your letter and I am sorry to hear about your shorts.

We certainly do have many of our customers wearing our garments

in any environment, so please be assured you do not have to wear

your shorts only at the beach.

If you would like me to see if there is a manufacturing fault with the shorts

could you please send a photo to our customer service email:

csc@billabonggroup.com.au and we will see what we can do for you.

I hope that helps with your enquiry however please feel free to call our

customer service department should you have any further enquires.

Kind Regards

Amy

Amy Easson | Customer Service Team Member |
Phone: 1300 301 453 | **Email:** csc@billabonggroup.com.au |

Billabong
1 Billabong Place
Burleigh Heads
QLD 4220

Neil Cameron
PO Box 6163
Yatala
QLD 4207

30-06-2014

Dear Amy

Photo? Um, is that even legal? Okay, well, so look, how about this— I will if you will. What do you reckon, shirts on, or shirts off? But for God's sake Amy please make sure you address yours to the attention of me — Mr Neil Cameron.

Yours slightly confused (but intrigued if I am totally honest)

Neil Cameron

PharmaCare Laboratories
Brut
18 Jubilee Ave
Warriewood
NSW 2102

Neil Cameron
PO Box 6163
Yatala
QLD 4207

03-06-2014

Dear Brut

My wife will not buy me any 'Brut Sport' Deodorant, (Heat Response). Because I do not play a sport. She said if I take up a sport, (she keeps suggesting Lawn Bowls ffs), I will be able to get some.

Look, could you write to her and tell her 'Brut Sport', (Heat Response), can still be used even if you do not play a sport?

This will save future arguments, (on this subject), and I can smell really nice for 48 hours. You can just write to me if you like and I will show her the letter. Be easier that way I think.

Thank you for helping me out on this one.

Yours sincerely

Neil Cameron

Neil Cameron
PO Box 6163
Yatala
QLD 4207

17th June 2014

Dear Neil,

Thank you for your letter regarding your wife's refusal to buy you Brut Sport Anti-Perspirant Deodorant.

We are both shocked and appalled, not only at Mrs. Cameron's belief that you need to play sport to feel the benefit of Brut Sport's excellent odour and sweat protection, but more so at her ongoing recommendation for Lawn Bowls.

Seriously, it's not even a sport. Unless it's Extreme Lawn Bowls and beer is involved.

We have attached a formal letter, detailing for Mrs. Cameron that she can, in good faith, purchase Brut Sport for you, without the need for you to actually play sport.

And we've included some Brut Sport to get you going.

I'm sure that once Mrs Cameron gets a whiff of the masculinity which is Brut, she'll be 'bowled' over too. Ha ha.

Yours sincerely

Ed Commander
Brut Snr. Brand Manager

PharmaCare Laboratories Pty Ltd. ABN 99 003 486 219 2102
T 02 9997 1465 F 02 9997 1698
Australia

18 Jubilee Avenue, Warriewood NSW

PO Box 384 Mona Vale NSW 1660

Mrs. Cameron
PO Box 6163
Yatala
QLD 4207

17th June 2014

A FORMAL LETTER FROM BRUT

Dear Mrs. Cameron,

This is to confirm that you can buy Brut Sport for your husband, Mr. Neil Cameron, without the need for him to actually play sport. Please buy Brut Sport for him in the future.

Just to set your mind at rest, we have included some Norsca Sport for you.

We can assure you, that you do not need to play any sport to enjoy Norsca Sport. If you are of a sporty nature, then we're sure you will enjoy Norsca Sport's superior protection.

Yours sincerely

Ed Commander

PharmaCare Laboratories Pty Ltd. ABN 99 003 468 219
2102
T 02 9997 1466 F 02 9997 1698
Australia

18 Jubilee Avenue, Warriewood NSW
PO Box 364 Mona Vale NSW 1660

NEIL CAMERON

PharmaCare Laboratories
Brut
18 Jubilee Ave
Warriewood
NSW 2102

Neil Cameron
PO Box 6163
Yatala
QLD 4207

11-07-2014

Dear Ed Commander (You made that up right?)

Thank you so much for the letter, samples and the letter of confirmation for the wife. She went and gave me a black eye and now I have to do the shopping. I smell bloody great while doing it though.

Yours thankfully?

Neil Cameron

Complaints Dept
Bundaberg Sugar
147 Wharf Street
Spring Hill
QLD 4000

Neil Cameron
PO Box 6163
Yatala
QLD 4207

17-05-2014

Dear Bundaberg Sugar

You sugar is too sweet. I bought a giant packet yesterday. Mistake! Why do you make it so sweet? Where I come from the sugar has just the right amount of sweetness.

What will you do to fix it?

Yours sincerely

Neil Cameron

Bundaberg Sugar Ltd
ABN 24 077 102 526

147 Wharf Street
Spring Hill Qld 4000

Tel: +61 (0)7 3835 8400
Fax: +61 (0)7 3835 8411
www.bundysugar.com.au

5th June 2014

Mr N Cameron
PO Box 6163
YATALA QLD 4207

Dear Neil,

Thank you for alerting us to the problem you experienced with our product. Bundaberg Sugar promptly responds to customer feedback as part of our efforts to satisfy our customers.

Your information has been forwarded to our Quality Personnel in an effort to identify the source of the problem. Where necessary we will change our procedures to prevent a recurrence of the problem you have brought to our attention. We apologise for any inconvenience caused and assure you of our commitment to the highest product and service standards.

If you require any additional information please do not hesitate to contact me on toll free 1800 777 097. Alternatively, I can be contacted by fax on (07) 3835 8411 or by e-mail: wbgrisda@bundysugar.com.au.

Kind regards,

Wayne Grisdale
National Sales Manager, Retail

Wayne Grisdale
Bundaberg Sugar
147 Wharf Street
Spring Hill
QLD 4000

Neil Cameron
PO Box 6163
Yatala
QLD 4207

17-06-2014

Dear Wayne

Hey no need to go bug your quality people, or even the not up to snuff ones —
I have just figured out to just use less. Sweet!

As you were Wayno, as you were.

Yours sincerely

Neil Cameron

NEIL CAMERON

Bunnings
National Support Centre
Locked Bag 3004
Hawthorn East
VIC 3122

Neil Cameron
PO Box 6163
Yatala
QLD 4207

20-05-2014

Dear Bunnings

It is a strange world we live in today. 'Greed is good' should be our motto, not 'God is good'. But anyway I want to talk to you about power tools today not the power of JC. More specifically post hole diggers. I bought one off you guys the other day.

I am building a fence to keep the dog & Nev the croc in. So I bought a post hole digger as I thought it would be easier than digging all the holes by hand.

I said to the Bunning's "lady" did she think I could operate the big post hole digger like the one I was pointing at on sale. I think she must have thought I was making a joke, and not a funny one either. She said her and her "partner" used one all the time on their property with no problems. She was the size of a gorilla though. I did not dare tell her that though. So I just bought the thing and prayed I could operate it.

This morning I had to go to the Emergency department at the hospital. Because your post hole digger, I bought yesterday, threw me against a tree, (a big one). I have sprained wrists, concussion, grazes and elongated arms.

I know when you make complaints like this that the person you are writing to is not normally at fault so I need you to know I have nothing against you. But the gorilla with the skin-head and eyebrow piercing I do. I just want you guys to be aware of her and her claims on big post hole diggers.

Also my mate Dave is going to build the fence now. So I want to bring the post hole digger back for a refund. It has a small paint chip on the handle. I know if I take it back to the shop they will say no because it has a small paint chip on the handle. Could you write me a letter for them saying to give me a refund because you know of the circumstances involved and it is all good? It would be less awkward all round for sure.

Thank you for this.

Yours sincerely

Neil Cameron

Mr. Neil Cameron
PO Box 6163
Yatala
QLD 4207

27 May 2014

Dear Mr. Cameron,

Thank you for your recent correspondence dated 20 May 2014, regarding the incident involving the post hole digger you purchased from Bunnings.

We are sorry to hear that the incident occurred, and hope that you are recovering well.

Bunnings are always concerned to hear of incidents involving its customers and thanks you for bringing the matter to our attention.

In order to assist you further, could you please contact me on 03 8831 9777.

Kind Regards,

Ashley Stewart
Customer Relations Officer

Bunnings Group Limited
ABN 26 008 672 179

A member of the Wesfarmers Limited
Group of Companies

16-18 Cato Street
Hawthorn East Australia 3123
Locked Bag 3004
Hawthorn Victoria 3122

Telephone +(61 3) 8831 9777
Facsimile +(61 3) 8831 9444
Website   www.bunnings.com.au

Complaints Dept
Coles Customer Care
PO Box 480
Glen Iris
VIC 3146

Neil Cameron
PO Box 6163
Yatala
QLD 4207

14-05-2014

Dear Coles

So yesterday I went to your store, (Coles). I always go on a Thursday. Thursday is the best time to go to Coles. Do not ask me why, it just is and we will leave it at that.

Your checkout staff, all they ever want to talk about is the weather. I do not want to talk about the weather. Yes I know they are stuck inside scanning groceries all day long so are interested in what the weather is like outside. Can they not just look out the windows? Does store policy not allow them? Why are they interested anyway, they are inside all day, what does it matter to them?

I am so tired of talking about the weather to Cole's checkout staff. Also they ask how I am, even though I can tell they do not care how I am, one way or another. I never ask them how they are. You know why? Because I do not care how they are. Just tell me how much I owe so I can get on my way please. So simple.

Tell me what you will do. Enough is enough I think you will agree.

Yours sincerely

Neil Cameron

coles

5 June 2014

Neil Cameron
PO Box 6163
YATALA QLD 4207

Dear Neil,

Thankyou for your letter dated May 20th.

We are sorry to hear of your dissatisfaction at the conversation which is often initiated by the checkout team member; it is certainly not our intention to annoy you.

However, while you may prefer not to converse with the team member during the checkout process, the vast majority of our customers appreciate a "Hello, how are you today" and some small talk, most consider this to be a common courtesy and are in fact offended if the team member does not speak to them.

While we are disappointed to learn of your dissatisfaction, we will continue to expect that our team members make contact with our customers, as we consider this to be conducive to good service.

Thank you again for taking the time to contact us, we appreciate your feedback and look forward to your future custom.

Yours sincerely

Imogen Connell
Coles Customer Care

Ref.   C092679350

Coles Group Limited ABN 11 004 089 936
800 Toorak Road Hawthorn East Victoria 3123 Australia
PO Box 2000 Glen Iris Victoria 3146 Australia
Telephone 1800 061 562 Facsimile 61 3 9829 3818
Website: www.coles.com.au

We will use your information for the purpose of recording your feedback and, if your feedback is product related, we may provide it to the supplier of the product. If you do not provide certain information that we request, we may not be able to fully assist you. Should you wish to see the personal information that we hold about you, please contact our Customer Care Contact Centre.

Imogen Connell
Coles Customer Care
PO Box 480
Glen Iris
VIC 3146

Neil Cameron
PO Box 6163
Yatala
QLD 4207

22-06-2014

Dear Imogen

The main problem is there is noise coming out of their cake-holes but there is no life coming out of their eye-balls.

I have some good ideas for you however. So stop panicking.

How about you train them to mumble incoherently or bark like a dog? Then put them through a training course on "How to Fake Interest in the Modern Era".

Get back to me on my ideas Imogen, (great ones, all of them),

Yours sincerely

Neil Cameron

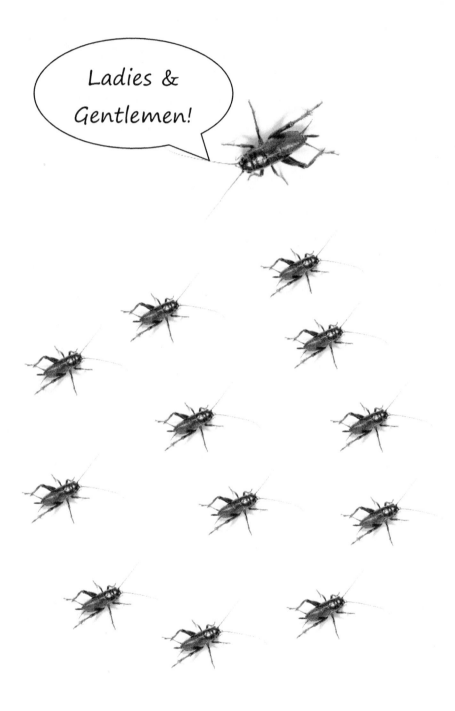

Lion Dairy & Drinks
Coon Cheese
737 Bourke Street
Docklandss
VIC 3008

Neil Cameron
PO Box 6163
Yatala
QLD 4207

18-09-2014

Dear Coon Cheese

We all know the jokes. They are pretty funny. Especially the one with the Jew in it.

I used to work with a bloke named Coon in The Netherlands, I have even seen a wild raccoon, I witnessed the annual Coon Carnival in Cape Town, you can buy black and tan Coon Hounds in America, I have even downloaded the original 1907 recording of 'If The Man in the Moon Were a Coon' sung by Ada Jones, I even have a friend from Switzerland who is a bona fide Coon. He is actually the reason for this letter.

He wants to see if I can track down any promotional material, such as posters, that feature your Swiss cheese. He would like to hang a few in his Cheese Shop in Bern. Would you be able to post me a few? I have written before about this but have not got a reply yet, (or any posters).

I look forward to hearing from you this time around.

Yours sincerely

Neil Cameron

NEIL CAMERON

+61 3 9188 6000
+61 3 9188 8001
www.lionco.com

Lion
737 Bourke Street
Docklands
VIC 3008
Australia

PO Box 23064
Docklands
VIC 8012
Australia

LD&D Australia Pty
Limited
ABN 68 063 010 290

Dear Neil,

Thank you for your letter.
I've been down into our
storage area + unfortunately
we don't have any LOON
merchandise or posters which
I can send you.

I thank you for your loyalty
+ hope you continue to
enjoy LOON cheese long into
the future.

Kind regards,
The LOON cheese team!

Lion Dairy & Drinks
Coon Cheese
737 Bourke Street
Docklandss
VIC 3008

Neil Cameron
PO Box 6163
Yatala
QLD 4207

04-10-2014

Dear The Coon Cheese team member with the hand-writing of a 7-year-old who can't quite write their name just yet.

Sorry to have made you walk all that way down to the Coon Cheese storage area, then all that way back up again- to your desk, chair, paper and your big boy/girl pen. I doubt it would have been a mile, but reading between the skewed lines it was evidently some form of extra effort. So, go you! Well done, have a piece of cheese.

Yours sincerely

Neil Cameron

Cottees Cordial
Customer Services
2 Beverage Drive
Tullamarine
VIC 3043

Neil Cameron
PO Box 6163
Yatala
QLD 4207

05-07-2014

Dear Cottees Cordial

My Dad never picked your fruit but I think his 2nd cousin might have.

But that is not the problem. I am the one with the problem. My driveway needs a sealing coat.

My mate Dave reckons your 'Coola lime' or your 'Pine Lime' would do the trick. He reckons the coal tar you add to them will seal my driveway a treat. He reckons not only will it seal my driveway it will give it a nice green hue.

Do you sell either in bulk? Say a 200ltr drum? How much? I will pay for shipping, do not worry on that score Cottees.

I look forward to your reply. Thank you.

Yours sincerely

Neil Cameron

Schweppes Australia Pty Ltd
ABN 31 024 243 998

Level 5, 111 Cecil Street
South Melbourne VIC 3205

PO Box 316
South Melbourne VIC 3205

Tel +61 3 8866 3888
Fax +61 3 8866 3879

schweppesaustralia.com.au

14 July 2014

Mr Neil Cameron
P O Box 6163
YATALA QLD 4207

Dear Neil,

Thank you for contacting us regarding Cottee's Cordials.

Please feel free to contact us on 1800-244-054 for any further product details.

Yours sincerely,
SCHWEPPES AUSTRALIA PTY LTD

Richard
Schweppes Consumer Relations

Ref. 0000183730

NEIL CAMERON

Cottees Cordial
Customer Services
2 Beverage Drive
Tullamarine
VIC 3043

Neil Cameron
PO Box 6163
Yatala
QLD 4207

21-07-2014

Dear Dicko

Thank you for contacting me after I contacted you.

As you can see I am now contacting you again.

I have contacted you again in the hope that you will contact me again.

Hopefully when you do make contact again it will mostly be concerning what I was contacting you about in the first place, (that I contacted you).

Please, please, please contact me again. Honestly Dick, I cannot wait.

Yours sincerely

Neil Cameron
P.S. I can be contacted at the above address, (just like when you contacted me the first time, do you remember?). If you want to contact me by phone, you can do that by sending me a God-damn fucking letter. Now look what you have made me do! You have got me fucking swearing! My Mum is going to end up reading this!

Heartland Didgeridoos
PO Box 257
Bellingen
NSW 2454

Neil Cameron
PO Box 6163
Yatala
QLD 4207

18-06-2014

Dear Heartland

I am not of Aboriginal decent but I do have a particularly large mouth. I know Rolf Harris originally had trouble getting his big ones blown properly and got away with small ones for years. However my request is the exact opposite, I can only play the bigger diameter didg. I do not like them covered in Beeswax. Like Rolf I like the feel of bare wood.

Do you stock such big didg's? Undecorated, as I have my own dot design. What about a custom made one?

Let me know your price. Thank you.

Peace my friend.

Yours sincerely

Neil Cameron

Neil Cameron
PO Box 6163
Yatala
QSLD 4207

11-7-2014

Hi Neil

So sorry for the delay in reply. Letters are obviously not my strong suit at the moment.

Thanks for your letter enquiring about support getting a special didgeridoo.

I can help you for sure with timber mouthpiece and larger hole, and to help me give you correct feedback on type and price, I really need to chat with you in person. Can you give me a call on 0488 559984.

I look forward to helping you,

All the best, Tynon

CONTACT- Tynon & Anthiam Bradford Alaom
PH/FAX- 02 6655 9881   EMAIL- tynon@heartdidg.com
SHOP ADDRESS – 2/25 Hyde St, Bellingen,
POST TO - PO Box 257, Bellingen,NSW,2454, AUSTRALIA
WEBSITE- www.heartdidg.com

Hills Hoist
Shared Services
Hills Ltd
159 Port Road
Hindmarsh
SA 5007

Neil Cameron
PO Box 6163
Yatala
QLD 4207

20-05-2014

Dear Hills Hoist

I need you to know that this is not an easy thing to talk about. So now you know.

I have a condition whereupon everyday life must be counter-clockwise. When people hear of my situation they think I am joking. Why would I? It is not funny. Basic day to day tasks are complicated and laborious. There are products on the market to help my kind already. Clocks, nuts and bolts to name a few.

Do you have a clothes line that will _only_ spin counter clockwise? Or could one be modified to achieve this? Maybe I could do this? (I am DIY handy).

In the windy conditions yesterday I had a panic attack and had to cut mine down with a hacksaw.

Thank you for listening.

Yours sincerely

Neil Cameron

HiLLS.

Hills Holdings Limited
ABN 35 007 573 417

159 Port Road
Hindmarsh
South Australia 5007

PO Box 922
Hindmarsh
South Australia 5007

T: +61 8 8301 3200
F: +61 8 8301 3300
info@hillsholdings.com.au

www.hillsholdings.com.au

27th May 2014

Neil Cameron,
Po Box 6163,
Yatala QLD 4207

Dear Neil,

Thank you for your letter about your Hills Hoist, I appreciate that it is not easy for you to share and I do appreciate your openness.

The extensive range of Rotary Hoists that we produce are all designed to move freely with wind assistance once they are wound-up above the wind brake, this enables the clothesline to spin in either a clockwise or counter clockwise direction and improves the drying efficiency.

We are not able to offer a modified Rotary Clothes hoist that would only spin in one direction, but we do have a range of Folding Frame Clotheslines that can be mounted on Posts or to a Wall and folded down flat when not in use, or a range of Extending Clotheslines that pull out of a Wall or Post mounted cabinet and extend to another wall or post.

If you do not want to change your style of Clothesline and wish to persist with a Rotary Clothesline, I can only suggest that you engage the Wind Brake when in use, this will stop it spinning altogether but will have an impact on the speed that your clothes dry with limited air movement around the washing hung out.

As a competent DIY handyman I'm sure that you would be able to construct something along the lines of a weather vane where the shape of the vane determines the movement that it takes, similar to a small concave sail.

I am sorry that I am not able to assist further with modifications to our Rotary Hoists and suggest that you view our extensive range of Clotheslines at http://www.hillshome.com.au/ for an alternate style that may suit your needs.

Kind Regards

Liam Johnston
Customer Service Manager

Patties Foods Operations
Four'n Twenty Pies
PO Box 409
Bairnsdale
VIC 3875

Neil Cameron
PO Box 6163
Yatala
QLD 4207

21-05-2014

Dear Four'n Twenty Pies

I am a sculptor. You have probably seen my work. My latest piece is an over-sized obese man in the midst of kicking a Sherrin AFL Ball. The entire sculpture will be made from pies on a wire frame. It will then be sprayed with a translucent resin to preserve and protect. It is entitled – 'I DID'. It will be on display outside the Adelaide Oval.

Can you supply me with any discount pie vouchers? Please let me know. Thank you in advance.

Yours sincerely

Neil Cameron

Patties Foods Ltd
ABN 62 007 157 182

Operations	Corporate Office
161-169 Princes Highway	Chifley Business Park
Bairnsdale VIC 3875	Level 2, 1 Joseph Avenue
PO Box 409	Mentone VIC 3194
Bairnsdale VIC 3875	PO Box 115
Phone: 03 5150 1800	Dingley VIC 3172
Admin Fax: 03 5152 1135	Phone: 03 8540 9100
Sales Fax: 03 5152 1054	Fax: 03 9551 3393
info@patties.com.au	Info@patties.com.au
www.patties.com.au	www.patties.com.au

28 May 2014

Dear Neil,

Thank you for your letter with regard to your request for discounted pie vouchers.

As we don't sell direct to the public and we have a varied chain of customers in both retail and petrol and convenience we don't offer direct discount vouchers.

Any potential brand association we would have with your sculpture would be misplaced as we don't supply Adelaide Oval one of our competitors in Balfours are the current supplier.

We wish you well in your piece of artwork.

Kind regards,

Lauren Boland
Events and Sponsorship Coordinator
Patties Foods Ltd

Lauren Boland
Patties Foods Operations
Four'n Twenty Pies
PO Box 409
Bairnsdale
VIC 3875

Neil Cameron
PO Box 6163
Yatala
QLD 4207

13-06-2014

Dear Lauren

I Googled your sentence —

"We wish you well in your piece of artwork"

Never before in the history of mankind, (or even Google), have these words been arranged in that order. Suggested search criteria however did contain all your words but also included these words — shit, shite, poo, poos, crap, crapola and steaming pile of do-do.

I really appreciate you taking the time to decline any pie vouchers and the not quite so veiled abuse of my life's work. Good stuff. You deserve a pie!

Yours sincerely

Neil Cameron

NEIL CAMERON

Audience & Consumer Affairs
GPO Box 9994
Brisbane
QLD 4001

Neil Cameron
PO Box 6163
Yatala
QLD 4207

18-09-2014

Dear ABC Audience & Consumer Affairs Mail Opener

I know you already have a big bag of complaints concerning the 'Jonah from Tonga' show. However I must add to it as I feel strongly about this "programme".

Lilley looks nothing like a 14-year-old Tongan boy. They have very large lips and a much darker skin tone not to mention a greater body mass. Which is due to their diet of coconuts, bananas and the super food - Taro. I know all of this for a fact as my best friend through school was Tongan. I have lost contact with him but I believe he has been in and out of gaol.

I think it is an outrage that you are depicting Tongans this way.

I know this type of cheap, controversial for controversial sake humour is aimed at the 14 to 15 year old market. But if you think about it that makes it just that little bit more shameful not to mention completely undemanding and sad. Lilley is the only one laughing here, (on his way to the bank).

What can be done about this farce? I need answers.

Yours sincerely

Neil Cameron

8 October 2014

ABC
Australian
Broadcasting
Corporation

Mr N Cameron
PO Box 6163
Yatala QLD 4207

ABC Ultimo Centre
700 Harris Street
Ultimo NSW 2007

GPO Box 9994
Sydney NSW 2001

Tel. +61 2 8333 1500
abc.net.au

Dear Mr Cameron

Thank you for your letter of 18 September regarding *Jonah from Tonga*.

I regret that you feel that Chris Lilley's portrayal of Jonah is outrageous. Please be assured your feedback has been noted by our unit and conveyed to ABC Television.

ABC Television advise:

"The character of Jonah Takalua is not intended to represent all Tongans but rather, an individually flawed, disenfranchised and troubled young man with extremely poor communication and decision making skills.

His conduct is the subject of intense scrutiny in the unfolding narrative which fully explores the impact on those directly affected by his behaviour and also the profound personal repercussions for Jonah himself.

Jonah's clear lack of respect toward his family and ignorance about his culture sits in stark contrast to those around him. These core deficiencies in Jonah's character provide the catalyst for a redemptive journey across the series.

While Jonah's starting point (and direct continuation from his previous appearance in the 2007 series, *Summer Heights High*, is abrasive and dismissive, by series end, his eyes are truly opened to the significance of family, culture and community.

Central to this journey is the character of Mr Fonua (aka Kool Kris), a proud Tongan man and inspirational youth worker who befriends Jonah and gradually instils in him a sense of pride, direction, self worth, spiritual awareness and greater purpose.

Throughout multiple series, Chris Lilley has displayed a unique skill in crafting highly individual characters that challenge and subvert preconceptions. We believe that Jonah Takalua is such a character.

The creative intention behind *Jonah from Tonga* is not to denigrate, but rather, to present a compelling and empathetic portrait of a deeply troubled young man in order to elicit a deeper examination and discussion into some of the more uncomfortable prejudices that exist in society today."

While Chris Lilley has altered his natural appearance to play the character of Jonah, it is important to note this is presented in a satirical context, and it does not follow that the program encourages or perpetuates racist or discriminatory attitudes."

Thank you once again for taking the time to write with your feedback.

Yours sincerely

Matthew Galvin
Audience and Consumer Affairs

2

ABC
Audience & Consumer Affairs
GPO Box 9994
Brisbane
QLD 4001

Neil Cameron
PO Box 6163
Yatala
QLD 4207

19-10-2014

Dear Mr Galvin

Bollocks.

Yours sincerely

Neil Cameron

NEIL CAMERON

TattsBet
PO Box 248
Albion
QLD 4010

Neil Cameron
PO Box 6163
Yatala
QLD 4207

07-06-2014

Dear TattsBet

I keep a couple of emus and every two weeks a bus load of Asian tourists stop to take photos of them in my back yard. You should see the little buggers run!

So it got me thinking about emu racing. So I built a little track yesterday and have four more emus coming next weekend. What I am going to do is charge the Asians two bucks a bet and the winner or winners can have a ride on one of the emus.

I know the bus driver as he has the odd beer down the pub. He reckons we would have time for three races. He said the bus is always full so that is about 63 Asians. So some good money to be made there.

My question is this - Would you guys have a problem with it? The emu racing that is.

Let me know so I can get the show on the road.

Yours sincerely

Neil Cameron

25 June 2014

Neil Cameron
PO Box 6163
YATALA QLD 4207

Dear Mr Cameron

Your proposed Emu Racing activities

I refer to your letter dated 20 May 2014 and apologise for the delay in responding.

We are intrigued and entertained by your proposal to conduct a little emu racing in your backyard. It sounds like it will be quite a sight!

We are aware that the Queensland Government is currently promoting Tourism as one of the four pillars of our economy, so we suggest that perhaps you might want to enquire with the relevant government department as to whether there would be any government funding for the development of your emu racing proposals. I'm sure the bus driver, as a potential beneficiary of your scheme, would be pleased to assist you with any such proposals.

As to whether TattsBet has any problem with your proposal to conduct emu racing in your backyard, we have no specific concerns at this time. You should seek your own legal advice regarding the legality of your proposal and check with the RSPCA and Biosecurity Queensland. You may wish to enquire with the Queensland Office of Liquor and Gaming Regulation to see whether they have any feedback about your intended activities. The best contact there would be Mr Michael Sarquis, Chief Executive, Queensland Office of Liquor and Gaming Regulation Locked Bag 180, City East, Qld 4002.

We wish you all the best in your future endeavours and thank for contacting us.

Have you tried the pies from Yatala Pie shop? It is famous and as I haven't stopped there for some years now, I must do so soon, but I am reliably informated that Emu pies are not available there.

Yours sincerely

Barrie Fletton
Chief Operating Officer

❖87 Ipswich Road, Woolloongabba 4102 Australia
❖Telephone (07) 3637 1400 ❖Facsimile (07) 3256 2373
TattsBet Limited ABN 84 085 691 738
A Tatts Group Company

Barrie Fletton
TattsBet
PO Box 248
Albion
QLD 4010

Neil Cameron
PO Box 6163
Yatala
QLD 4207

08-07-2014

Dear Baz

Emu pies? You might be on to something there bud. I will get the wife to cook up some chicken ones, they will never know the difference. Hell they have a soft spot for Alsatian right?
Yatala Pies, exit 38 mate, exit 38. Tell them Neil Cameron sent you.

Nice one Barrie.

Yours sincerely

Neil Cameron

Victoria Racing Club
448 Epsom Road
Flemington
VIC 3031

Neil Cameron
PO Box 6163
Yatala
QLD 4207

03-05-2014

Dear Victoria Racing Club

I received some very sad news yesterday. My good mate Gordon is slowly dying. He is like that old saying —"One in a million" probably more.

He just loved to run and boy was he fast! He won three races on the trot but had eight DNF's after that. The Vet said Gordon was completely blind in his left eye. The three wins were all on counter clockwise tracks. We got the Vet in again yesterday.

I promised Gordon I would make him a champion. We had our sights set on The Melbourne Cup. Because he is blind in his left eye and is going to die that will not happen now. I feel like I have let my mate down.

Would it be okay if I bring Gordo over to Flemington for a lap? The last week next month would suit us fine. What about you? He is not contagious or anything.

Hope you can help us. Gordon is a great horse. Look forward to meeting you.

Yours sincerely

Neil Cameron

NEIL CAMERON

27 May 2014

Mr N Cameron
PO Box 6763
Yatala QLD 4207

Dear Neil,

Thank you for your letter in relation to your good mate Gordon, he does sound like a very special horse.

The VRC has strict regulations around the use of the Flemington Racetrack; unfortunately it saddens me to advise that we cannot be of help in accommodating your request. Access to the Flemington Racetrack is reserved strictly for Flemington trained horses and horses required in extra special ceremonial events.

We wish you and Gordon all the best for his remaining time.

Yours sincerely

Mick Goodie
Flemington Racecourse Manager

 victoria racing club

www.flemington.com.au

Emirates
Principal Partner

Victoria Racing Club Limited (ACN 119 214 078)   448 Epsom Road Flemington VIC 3031
Phone: Head Office (+ 61 3) 8378 0888 Customer Service 1300 727 575 Racecourse (+ 61 3) 9371 7171
Facsimile: Customer Service (+ 61 3) 8378 0855 Racecourse (+ 61 3) 9376 9273
Email Customer Service: customerservice@vrc.net.au

Mick Goodie
Victoria Racing Club
448 Epsom Road
Flemington
VIC 3031

Neil Cameron
PO Box 6163
Yatala
QLD 4207

04-06-2014

Dear Mr Goodie

I shot him.

Yours sincerely

Neil Cameron

NEIL CAMERON

City of Sydney
Sydney Harbour Bridge
GPO Box 1591
Sydney NSW 2001

Neil Cameron
PO Box 6163
Yatala
QLD 4207

23-05-2014

Dear City of Sydney

I am going to set a new world record — 'The first man to Pogo backwards blind-folded over the Sydney Harbour Bridge'. I have contacted Guinness.

Two Doco Cameramen, my Manager, a Paramedic and an official from Guinness, (Guinness requirement), would need to accompany me during the record attempt. Ladders and stairs are no barrier.

We have pencilled in the last week in November for the attempt. Does that suit you guys?

Look forward to working with you in this world record attempt!

Yours sincerely

Neil Cameron
(Pro-Pogo Stuntman)

City of Sydney
Town Hall House
456 Kent Street
Sydney NSW 2000

Telephone +61 2 9265 9333
Fax +61 2 9265 9222
council@cityofsydney.nsw.gov.au

GPO Box 1591 Sydney NSW 2001
cityofsydney.nsw.gov.au

14-Jul-2014

Neil Cameron
PO BOX 6163
YATALA QLD 4207

Dear Neil,

To make arrangements for your plan to be the first man to Pogo backwards blind-folded over the Sydney Harbour Bridge, you will need to contact RMS (Roads and Maritime Services) which operates and maintains the Sydney Harbour Bridge for the New South Wales State Government which owns the bridge : please see the following link:
http://www.rms.nsw.gov.au/roadprojects/cgi-bin/index.cgi?action=feedback.form&path=/roadprojects/contactus

The following links may be of interest to you:
* http://www.rta.nsw.gov.au/roadprojects/projects/shb_precinct/shb_80th/index.html
* http://www.rta.nsw.gov.au/roadphttp://www.rms.nsw.gov.au/roadprojects/cgi-bin/index.cgi?action=feedback.form&path=/roadprojects/contactusrojects/projects/shb_precinct/history.html

Kind regards,

Customer Service Centre
City of Sydney
Tel: 02 9265 9333
Fax: 02 9265 9222
www.cityofsydney.nsw.gov.au

Green. Global. Connected | www.sydney2030.com.au
Integrity. Innovation. Collaboration. Courage. Quality. Respect
Please consider the environment before printing this email.

CITYOFSYDNEY

NEIL CAMERON

Myer Support office
800 Collins Street
Docklands
Melbourne
VIC 3008

Neil Cameron
PO Box 6163
Yatala
QLD 4207

04-05-2014

Dear Myers

Straight off this maybe weird for you. For me it is just a normal hobby and everyone should keep their noses out of my business anyway, (like both neighbours).

So my hobby is the collection of female mannequins. Vintage ones for the most part. I was in Myers yesterday and saw your fat female mannequins. Wow-wow-we! I have never seen fat female mannequins before! I am really interested in getting my hands on one. Do you have any old or even damaged fat female mannequins that you want to get rid of? I can pay for one if you want. How much money would you want for one or maybe even two fat ones? Even if a fat arm or a fat leg is missing. I will pay for shipping or I will hire a little truck if it is close enough.

Really hope you can help me build up my female mannequin collection. Look forward to hearing from you!

Please help!

Yours sincerely

Neil Cameron

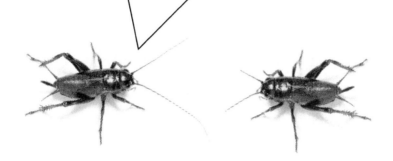

ABOUT THE AUTHOR

Neil Cameron was born totally free from any form of – talent, sporting ability, family fortune, good looks, good health or luck, (the good sort). Ask his Mum, she will tell you. He spends his days, (and most nights), writing copious letters to anyone and everyone. Thus keeping his hands busy and away from sharp instruments, nooses, giant wooden crucifixes, hammers, nails, bottles of sleeping pills, guns and explosives.

Please do not attempt to contact Neil Cameron via his Yalata post box. It's under surveillance, (also he hasn't paid his bill). Neil is currently on the run, (counter-clockwise, always), living out of his trusty rusty HQ wagon, with only a pilfered fat one-armed mannequin for company. Try neil.camerons.email@gmail.com
Even though he is very hungry, very tired and flat broke, (very), he will get back to you...eventually. However, if you have money, (a surplus), he will respond immediately.

Volume 2

The Camel saga continues

Jetstar

Milo

Optus

Rip Curl

The Wiggles

Woolworths

Twisties

Vegemite

Ugg Boots

Speedo

And many more!

Acknowledgments

Shutterstock - Cover photo

Zdenek Sasek - Stickman artwork

The South African - Everything else

Printed in Great Britain
by Amazon

14781223R00051